RELIG

ISLAM
RELIGION OF LIFE

Dr Abdul Wadod Shalabi
President of the Supreme Commission
for Islamic Da'wa
Al-Azhar

The Quilliam Press
1989

© Abdal Wadod Shalabi, 1989

First published in 1986 by
Al-Azhar, Cairo, Egypt

This edition published 1989 by
The Quilliam Press Limited,
Tanglewood House, Dorton,
Buckinghamshire, England

ISBN 1 872038 02 6

Text edited by A.H. Murad

Printed in England by
Piggott Printers Ltd, Cambridge

CONTENTS

Foreword

The university of al-Azhar, the world's oldest academic institution, recently celebrated its first millennium; and the spectacular celebrations, in which many of the Muslim world's greatest stars participated, reaffirmed al-Azhar's continuing dynamism and central importance for the Islamic intellectual tradition. It showed that in every Muslim country, thousands of Azhari graduates continue to look to Cairo for inspiration, new ideas, and doctrinal authority.

Shaikh Abdul Wadod Shalabi is proof of this resilience. The author of over twenty books on all aspects of Islam, he combines a deep loyalty to his Azhari theological training with an acute understanding of the crisis of the modern world. His studies abroad, which earned him a doctorate from the University of Cambridge, and his prominent career in the Azhar hierarchy (he has been editor of its journal, and deputy Shaikh of the Azhar), have put him in a unique position to assess and criticise the forces of Westernisation which are undermining the culture, faith and morality not just of Egypt but of every Muslim land.

The present work grew out of a series of English-language radio broadcasts, the popularity of which encouraged the author to create this book. Although designed as a general introduction to the Islamic faith, its insights into what one might term the "spiritual metabolism" of the Muslim way of life are profound, and bear witness to the wisdom, tolerance and deep piety of its author.

Layla Sabah

Preface

The breaking of an image

Islam: a word to conjure with. Veiled women, the oil weapon, holy war. One thousand million human beings crammed together under one journalistic label. The unchanging, sensuous, puritanical East of Flaubert and Montesquieu, translated into the language of the media: a potent political weapon. A world of peoples, cultures and dreams, transmuted into an abstraction, an alien threat, a monolith.

This image of "Islam" now forms a key part of the Western world's collective consciousness. Violence, obscurantism, and the unaccountable desire of non-European peoples to live as they choose, all these are disturbing facts which are less disturbing when put down to something called Islam, an abstraction whose basic features, fused with an ancient substratum of medieval fear, are never called into question. Muslims act as they do because they are Muslims, not because they are human beings with whom the consumers of the mass media can identify. The image is closed: aberrations in the Muslim world are the result of something called "Islam"; "Islam" is therefore aberrant, unintelligible, and all that is evil can be laid at its door without endangering the principles of the most liberal journalist.

This book is written about Islam from within. It seeks to show something of the true nature of the faith, thereby challenging the accepted stereotypes

1

which so badly compromise the present dialogue of civilisations. By explaining the significance of the formal practices and doctrines of the Islamic religion it endeavours to build a bridge over what must be the deepest yet most irrational gulf ever to have cleaved apart two cultures.

Introduction

The starting-point of any religion is wonderment. The sheer mystery of our lives demands an explanation. From the gas clouds floating in interstellar space to the tiniest subatomic particles, the realm of action into which we have been thrust must be understood if we are to know how to live. "The unexamined life is not worth living," said Socrates, and this question is always true, always equally urgent. Religion, as the only means of finding an answer to this question, is thus the most important, indeed, in a sense, the only meaningful activity of man.

Philosophy reaches upwards and is frustrated. Religion reaches downwards from Heaven, and, if not corrupted at the hands of men, can bring us to a true understanding of ourselves and our function. And it is not inaccessible: for in every nation in history prophetic figures have arisen, calling men to purity, sainthood, and salvation. True, their messages have differed. True, they have at times given rise to intolerance and war. But enough is visible still of their initial teachings for us to conclude that the founders of the great religions of mankind shared in a common vision, an experience of that absolute state of beyond-being which in the English language we call God.

The consciousness shared by the prophets and saints of history necessarily expressed itself in terms which best conveyed it in a rich variety of cultural worlds. But with the inauguration of each new

3

revelation the same energy was at work, the Divine secret called by some the Logos, by others the Light of Muhammad: the uncreated point of contact between the Absolute and the contingent, the Creator and the created. According to the teachings of the most recent manifestation of this force in the person of the Prophet of Islam, there have been throughout history no fewer than one hundred and twenty-four thousand such figures. Some were to found religions, others merely revived sacred traditions already present in their worlds, but in every case the transformative experience of God was the same.

The process of revelation added a dimension essential to the structure of the created world. Just as the universe comprises a system of opposites: light and darkness, up and down, dense and subtle, the intervention of the Transcendent introduced the opposition of "gravity and grace", or materialism as opposed to a concern with meaning and spiritual insight. The focus of this new contrast was man, who, because of the determining importance of the religious project, became the cornerstone of the universe.

Central to man's metaphysical role is his understanding that although he constitutes the potential point of transition between God, Who is beyond his comprehension, in that He is pure Unity and is only knowable to Himself, and the created world which is the necessary realm of total possibility implicit in that Unity, he is bound by his material nature to the tangible. To know God is to renounce the world only in its worldliness; it does not imply a rejection of being human. To the man of religious insight, the world is a realm of trial, of self-purification and of austerity, but it is not intrinsically evil, since it is of God. This understanding forms the basis of the normative religious project.

From this it is clear that every religious creed must have two fundamental elements. Firstly, it must affirm the absolute unity of the Transcendent; and secondly, it must affirm the existence of a way of life which reflects this unity and assists mankind to draw near to it. In the context of Islam, this creed is called the Dual Testimony, that there is no deity save God (*la ilaha illa'Llah*) and that Muhammad is His final Messenger (*Muhammadun rasulu'Llah*). In other words, we are speaking of doctrine and practice.

Before looking in more detail at this dual formulation, it is necessary to examine the question of religious exclusivity. We have already said that Islam is the last of the great world religions, and the implications of this for the way Muslims see other religious faiths are wide-ranging. Of the three traditions of Middle Eastern origin, Judaism has historically restricted its message to the Jewish people, and has regarded with scepticism the claims of Jesus and Muhammad to be new manifestations of the divine scheme of revelation and guidance. Similarly, Christians have throughout their history rejected the prophetic status of Muhammad: Catholic theology traditionally consigns Abraham to purgatory and Muhammad to the Inferno, along with his followers. But Islam, coming after its two great predecessors, was able to recognise the genuineness of the Prophetic mission of the Jewish prophets and of the Messianic status of Jesus Christ.

But at this point a question must be asked. Granted that Muslims recognise the authenticity of their predecessors' messages, why the need for a new religious dispensation at all? If the teachings of Jesus, for example, are true, and bring salvation, then why should it be necessary to follow anyone else?

The answer lies in humanity's development as this has taken place through history. The religious system given to the wandering tribes at the time of Abraham was tailored to its age and to a certain set of cultural circumstances. With the advent of classical civilisation this system stood in need of rearticulation in a language intelligible in the Graeco-Roman world. And when this world declined, and was replaced by new civilisations, the revelation of Islam was inaugurated.

In this sense there is no such thing as a new religion. Eternal truth, in order that it may be fully understood, must present itself differently to different worlds. Thus Islam, despite certain real but superficial differences, is also the faith of Jesus, Abraham and Moses.

A further point needs to be made. Not only did the course of ancient history necessitate a sequence of revelations; it also demanded that the scope, as well as the cultural content of the new dispensations had to alter. The ancient religions, such as Hinduism and Judaism restricted their message to a single geographical or racial group. With the dawning of the Axial Age and the great world civilisations of antiquity the new revelations became more universal in their scope. And at the critical point when the classical world broke down, at the close of the ancient order

and the dim opening of the new, at the very beginning of the unprecedented chain of events which was
to give birth to the modern world, the Prophet
Muhammad was born. This book explains, in an
unavoidably condensed fashion, what he had to say.

Chapter One

The Testimonies of Faith

La ilaha illa'Llah: there is no deity save God.
Muhammadun rasulu'Llah: Muhammad is the
messenger of God.

These two phrases, which punctuate and transform
the Muslim life, sum up fully the theology of the
Islamic religion. By implication more than by statement: the First Testimony declares the unity of the
metaphysical, while the second is the gate to what
that unity implies.

No deity save God: pure monotheism. No object of
worship save God, no conditioner of meaning apart
from Him. An affirmation of complete tran-
scendence; the most perfect articulation of what lies
forever beyond the reach of language.

Prophethood: the road to affirmation and recog-
nition of ultimate participation in that Unity.
Through the course of history the veil is torn, and the
supernal light washes clean some human soul. A
religion is born. A nation for God is founded. A
sacred civilisation saves millions of souls from life on
the horizontal, from the profane, from the banal.

Full membership of the world community of Islam
consists in the uttering of these two statements.
Nothing more, nothing less. There is no rite of
initiation, no sacrament of belief. It is a faith of the
individual, which transforms societies. And a faith

without intermediaries, without the spiritual broker-age of a priestly class. The experience of the Light of Muhammad which is the line between the absolute and the contingent is not monopolised by a formal hierarchy of clergymen, rather it cascades historically from the Prophets to the generations of mankind through men and women who by their own spiritual strivings rather than through any formal liturgical function are inwardly invested as saints.

But religions, like human beings, enjoy a natural span of life. The enthusiasm of youth is, with the passing of the years, supplanted by the maturity and sophistication of middle age, until finally the fits and distractions of senility presage what may be a long twilight. As the distance between the inaugural surge of revelatory wisdom and the latest generation of believers grows wider, the intensity of religious experience naturally wanes. Heresy, always accom-panied by spiritual impoverishment, begins to flour-ish. Orthodoxy, increasingly crippled by its ins-titutions, loses its intellectual and moral author-ity. The material concerns of the community, tradi-tionally quite legitimate, grow out of proportion at the expense of faith and morality. Thus a downward spiral gathers pace until religion becomes no more than a source of embarrassment in a world where its language has been reduced and corrupted by mat-erial values to no more than a vehicle for sentimen-tality.

The chain of transmission between revelation and the moment, or between the metaphysical confession of faith and its practical implications, may periodi-cally be reforged by a saint. Yet in every case the reversal is incomplete. In the Christian world today there is no saint who in wisdom and gentleness can stand comparison with the Apostles. There is no Hindu guru of the calibre of the companions of Krishna. And in the context of Islam, as the Blessed Prophet affirmed: "The best of generations shall be my own, and then that which follows, and then that which follows again."

Spiritual entropy: the backbone of history. A dialectic far more profound and exact than the dialectical materialism of the Marxist, who sees the process from beneath, as it were, and imagines it to be grounds for optimism. Religion is intensely realistic, not utopian. The millennium can never be wrought by human hands alone: without faith man will always tend to selfishness and strife; rather, the kingdom of God on this earth, as promised by every revealed religion, will be an act of unmerited grace, an age of peace established as a respite in the violent days before man's story draws to a close.

Religion, then, when seen in the context of the Two Testimonies, recognises man's essential inability to deal with his world. A social contract based on belief in spiritual growth and final judgement is the best foundation for a caring society. Wherever this belief is strong, and this of necessity becomes increasingly rare, then alone can man hope to become what Muslims call God's viceroy, his *khalifa* on the earth. But this status, which is what we were created to strive for, nevertheless recognises that man cannot deal with his situation unaided. Outside help is indispensable.

The medieval Muslim philosopher of Spain, Ibn

Tufail, sought to approach this problem by means of a parable. He tells the story of a child stranded on a desert island, who, without even the benefit of language, grows into manhood. In his quiet and idyllic isolation he is able to think deeply and without prejudice about the signs of nature and beauty which surround him, and he comes to the conclusion that only a good and omnipotent First Cause could account for what he sees. With this natural theology, with this strong and unaffected faith, the young man discovers the ideal way to live in his small world, a style of life in which every action reflects joyfully and spontaneously his love of his Creator. And when at last he is rescued by a ship of Muslim sailors, he recognises Islam to be none other than that *élan* for dealing with the world which he had found within himself.

The Two Testimonies of Islam imply of necessity the existence of this fundamental stratum of faith in the human consciousness. The Qur'an calls it man's *fitra*, his "natural disposition", which is to love God, beauty, and all men, and to feel revulsion towards selfishness, ugliness and evil. Muslim ethical thought starts with this assumption, that man is fundamentally a creature of goodness and faith, and that, as the Prophet said, "every child is born with the *fitra*", and that evil is only the product of his environment and upbringing. This is one implication of every religion's affirmation that man is created in God's image: goodness is an attribute of the Absolute, while evil belongs to the realm of the contingent, which is by its own nature impermanent.

"There is no deity save God" is thus the foundation of every human personality. Upon this foundation are heaped the accretions of years of neglect and foolishness; yet religious knowledge is still a possibility for all men. Fundamental goodness in this sense negates the Christian doctrine of original sin: evil is from one's world, not from one's soul, which is of God.

Ibn Tufail's parable shows that man is, in his natural state, in harmony with God and the created world over which he has been given authority. Yet the harsh realities of the world are usually quite different. Man is evidently not in harmony with anything. Wars, injustices and intolerance are the rule rather than the exception. Distance from the sources of revelation brings about a kind of hardening in the spiritual ether; tyranny becomes more usual than tranquillity. This is not to say that the religious project has failed, however; it merely means that it has become the concern of individuals rather than societies. And indeed we see that the older and more ineffectual a religious tradition becomes, the more it relinquishes its claims to a conditioning role in the political and social process.

However strong his faith in God's unity and presence may be, no individual believer is likely to design for himself and for his society a pattern of worship and behaviour which fully reflects and affirms it. In addition, faith in a God Who takes a total interest in the affairs of His creatures leads us intellectually to ask certain further questions relating to our relationship with Him. How may we approach Him, and come to know Him more fully? What is the true nature of the human soul? What was its nature before our birth, and what, if any, will be its fate after death?

These and other questions are addressed by the Second Testimony of Islam. Muhammad is the Messenger of God. In other words, he carries with him a message. He confirms what was taught by every prophet before him, and clarifies much that was previously unknown. At the forefront of his teachings comes the reminder that the universe has a Cause, and that this Cause is One. Secondly, he reminds us that we must affirm this realisation in our lives. In order to make this easier he has been given a set of devotional practices, the most important of which are known as the 'pillars of Islam', which constitute the ideal and most simple means of approaching God. Thirdly, he tells us of God's will regarding the most successful organisation of human society along lines that will create a suitable environment for the religious project. This system is known in Arabic as the *Sharia*, the Way. And in addition to all this, he tells us of the spiritual world, of the Angels, the other worlds, and of the end of time: the Apocalypse foretold by every religion, when all mankind shall be judged.

Muhammad is the Messenger of God: a metaphysical statement, but also a historical one. Religions should be judged by their fruits, by their capacity to produce sainthood, by their contribution to the spiritual life of mankind. But to accept a religion is more easy if its origins in time are understood. Every faith mediates itself in terms of symbols revolving around the life of its founder, whose qualities, and whose teachings and miracles, made such a profound impact on the lives of those who kept his company.

No deity but God; Muhammad is His Messenger. Where were these words first spoken, which probably have changed history more than any other? And how does this formulation supplant the pre-Islamic faiths?

When Islam burst upon the seventh-century Arabian peninsula the Arab tribes were living in a state of neolithic ignorance. Wandering clans, constantly in a state of internecine warfare, each boasted of an idol, a god of stone or wood. But scattered over these spiritual deserts there lived a small number of men, ascetics dwelling in distant tents or caves, who called themselves *hunafa*, those of unpolluted faith. They knew that Ishmael, ancestor of the Arabs - the Midianites or Ishmaelites of the Bible - had worshipped One God, and Him alone. They had watched in sorrow the falling away of the sons of Ishmael from the pure teachings of Abraham, and had looked on as pagan deities were gradually adopted among the tribes, until even the sacred temple Abraham had built at Mecca was degraded into a pagan sanctuary.

Further north, the tribes of Israel had long been in spiritual decline also. The image of the angered Yahweh of Isaiah and Jeremiah declaring that "Your forefathers have abandoned Me and have followed other gods, worshipping them and bowing down before them" is a moving reminder that Judaism had fallen victim to hierophancy, the tyranny of a priestly elite ruling the so-called "chosen people" through an elaborate and artificial Law far removed from the open and simple code of life which Moses had received on Sinai.

Jesus who, as the Evangelist records, "came not to

destroy the Law but to fulfill it", created a small but rapidly expanding community of Jews fired by his messianic energy to revive the fossilised Law and to invest it with new meaning. But as his teachings took root in the Hellenistic "culture compost" of the Roman East they soon diverged into sects of radically differing outlooks. The belief of apostolic Christianity, as modern church historians tell us, was a pure monotheism. Belief in the divinity of Jesus and in the redemptive sacrifice at Calvary was present only in the Hellenistic sects, under the influence of the Greek and very un-Semitic notion of incarnation, mutated strangely by the atonement cults of Osiris and Mithras. But by the year 315 the Greek Christians had received official favour: the Emperor Constantine the Great embraced their creed, and summoned the Council of Nicea to declare the Trinity, not the Unity of God, to be the only legal faith of the Roman empire. Over three million monotheist Christians were subsequently put to the sword for holding to what they considered to be Jesus's original teachings of the absolute unity of God. The persistent recurrence of belief in a pure monotheism in the Arian movement reveals just how strong was aversion to the new orthodoxy.

Then, in the early seventh century, when Christianity seemed drowned in the dark ages of sectarianism and decay, Islam shone forth from the land of Ishmael. Its teachings were blindingly simple: the uncompromising unity of God, and man's duty to live for others. The Middle East, tired of hairsplitting debates on the respective natures of the Father, the Son and the Holy Ghost, welcomed this new creed wholeheartedly, joyfully recognising the same simple and godly qualities that had made Jesus change their lives in the person of the new Arabian Prophet. "La ilaha illa 'Llah", the ancient world suddenly proclaimed. An end to corrupt and exploitative bishops. An end to a theology which left men in puzzlement and bloody schism. Everywhere, humanity responded to God's new word, and flocked in love and humility to the envoys of Islam wherever they penetrated.

It is surely one of the greatest miracles of history that from the backwater of Arabia there should have exploded a group of men, companions of a Prophet, who within the space of a few brief decades were able to create a magnificent civilisation extending from the Pyrenees to the gates of China. The dynamic which brought about this miracle was the Two Testimonies of Islam, as expounded in a book of unprecedented beauty and power called the Qur'an. Even more astonishing is the fact that this remarkable transformation came about peaceably. The Byzantine historians record of the Muslims an almost miraculous degree of religious toleration during this period, for the Muslims were deeply immersed in the Qur'anic spirit of tolerance which declares: "There shall be no compulsion in religion." It is almost impossible for the modern mind to comprehend some of the actions of the early Companions. When the caliph Omar heard that a church had been demolished by a group of Muslims in the distant Syrian mountains and a mosque erected in its stead he grew angry, and issued an order for the demolition of the mosque, and commanded the renegade tribesmen responsible to rebuild the church with their own hands. The Christian clergy wrote with astonishment of the new spirit of brotherhood which filled the East after the retreat of the Byzantines, long resented for their extortionate taxes and religious intolerance towards the Monophysite and Arian churches. The Muslim world became a place of refuge for all manner of religious dissent in Europe: Arians, Cathars, Jews.

A thousand years on, the Muslim world enjoyed the same spirit of tolerance, when during the happy days of Turkish rule in the Balkans whole villages were established there by Unitarian and Calvinist dissidents. History hardly bears out the prejudice still common in the West that Islam is to be dismissed as a religion of scimitar-waving fanatics; rather it is Europe, the land of the Inquisition, the Crusades, and the rape of the Americas, which emerges with the more sanguinary record.

Islam's tolerance springs in fact from the pluralistic vision of the Qur'an. As we have already seen, Muslims recognise the genuineness of the messages given to Moses and Jesus, and allow them to live in accordance with their own beliefs. To demolish a church or a synagogue, or to convert such a building into a mosque, is almost impossible under Islamic law. Thus Christian communities still flourish in the Arab world more than fourteen hundred years after the appearance of Islam; yet one is permitted to ask, how many Muslims were suffered to remain in Andalusia after the Catholic Reconquest?

That the message of Islam should have proved so popular, however, demands an explanation more exact. To account for the Muslim explosion in terms of political advantage is to deride the integrity of the human spirit, while to put it down to superior theology is to accord that same spirit more skill in discrimination than it usually seems to display. Most people judge a religion by its practical effects on the lives of those who practice it, and this attitude undoubtedly does much to explain why wherever Muslim travellers and merchants penetrated, they left in their wake communities of new believers. Far outside the limits of Islam's political sway convert communities soon established themselves, in cities as remote as Budapest and Shanghai.

The early Muslim voyagers were in many cases saintly men. Their mere presence profoundly impressed those who saw them or had dealings with them. But even the ordinary believer was clearly possessed of qualities which set him apart from others. His honesty, gentleness and kindness to children excited curiosity and respect. His was a tranquillity balanced by action: a life as industrious as it was prayerful. His cities contained places of worship of the most sublime peace and symmetry, and also lively markets built right up to their walls: a perfect symbol of his society and of his vision of the universe.

This equilibrium of character was the consequence of the subtle interplay of a variety of factors which resulted from the internalisation of the Qur'anic message. The most immediately felt impact of his faith on the newcomer to Islam is invariably a sense of finding a place in the cosmos, which now divides itself into good and evil. The value of his life is immediately measurable by his intellect and spirit in terms of its conformity to God's will, as we are reminded of it in the Qur'an.

The Muslim personality is characterised by another advantage. The conviction that absolute truth is to be discovered through a certain way of life inspires an emotion of true freedom and independence. Obedience is due to God alone, and no man can hold mental sway over the believer. And as he learns to discipline himself in accordance with God's will he begin to free himself from the blind dictates of the body, which always cries out for immediate gratification of the need for food and sex. The believer is enabled to control his physical form rather than be controlled by it. This quality, which is a prerequisite for spiritual growth, is also of inestimable worth in pursuing one's material interests.

Life in the Two Testimonies of Islam inspires courage and dynamism. Ours is a faith of works. In other words, salvation in the life to come is not achieved solely through verbal assent to a doctrine, but rather may only be assured by acting to the best of one's abilities in the way which best serves mankind and the spiritual life which alone conditions life with meaning. The Muslim is thus the man of simultaneous stillness and movement.

Yet another mundane benefit arising from the Muslim's religious orientation is the knowledge and certainty that all that takes place in his daily round is by God's leave. He is thus enabled to meet any misfortune which may overtake him far more stoically than the man of weak faith, for he knows that all things are by the will of God, which is the unfolding of His knowledge, and that, as the Prophet said: "When God loves His servant, He sends trials upon him". Every misfortune thus takes on an aspect of purification and atonement rather than being the inexplicable and random operation of fate. This is not to be confused with the traditional belief held by many Westerners that Islam is a religion of fatalism and apathy, for the Muslims are constantly exhorted by the Qur'an to act. Rather it constitutes a means of consolation for those whose faith is pure, and who perceive the workings of Providence in all the vicissitudes of life.

Taking on the world-view of Islam has still another positive implication, one which is political in nature and today highly controversial. For the Muslim, his belief leaves no room for arrogance and the lust for power; indeed, he is enjoined to stand out against tyranny and injustice wherever he encounters it. The ungodly mind is always driving for the acquisition of absolute authority, which for the believer is the prerogative of God alone. Thus the Muslim is active not only in the mosque but also in the corridors of power, seeking whenever he can to combat injustice and corruption from within the political processes already in motion. Whenever he can, also, he endeavours to establish a government which sees itself as the mere representative of a higher power, a government whose movements are kept within the precincts of justice by its necessary commitment to the ethical ideals laid down by God Himself. For Islam is a complete system of individual and collective life. There is no division between the sacred and the secular. The world is a manifestation of the attributes of the Divinity, and every human activity must ultimately reflect this. Islam provides man with a spiritual technology by which he may come to know his Creator, thereby fulfilling the function for which he was made, and it is precisely because this process is of such overriding importance that the function of society must rise above that of the provision of man's material needs and must seek to provide him with the best possible environment in which to carry out this project of self-discovery and realisation. Thus Islam's concern with politics. The quest for salvation and grace must take precedence over, and absorb and sanctify, the collective material endeavours of mankind.

It might be argued that a religion, although capable of transforming societies through a fixed outward blueprint which reflects the inward questing of its adherents, must be prepared to adopt new moral and social structures if it is to maintain its relevance to a changing world. Religion should not seek to "turn the clock back", we are told. After all, is it not Islam's claim that the religions which predated it lost their immediate appropriateness to their cultures when these decayed or were mutated by outside influences? Similarly, is it credible to assert that the Islamic vision, with its legal system and social norms, is truly universal, that it is workable in every land under the sun?

The Muslim world's response to this accusation is a unanimous yes. One of the most astonishing miracles of Islam is that despite its all-encompassing nature, through which it lays down guidance for every aspect of human life, it has never proved impracticable in any place, or at any point throughout its long and complex history. As we have said, Islam lays down instructions to ensure the fair and effective operation of government. It explains and regulates the function of wealth in an economy. It shows how to organise a contented society based on a firm commitment to the family. It tells us to investigate the world around us and to fathom its secrets. Yet despite this wealth of guidance, no Muslim on the face of the earth today can say that his faith is not practicable in the particular situation in which he or she has been set.

Islam's universal mission was proclaimed and inaugurated at the very beginning of its story by the Prophet Muhammad, who proclaimed to the astonished and derisory tribesmen of Mecca: "I am the Messenger of God now sent to you, and to humanity at large." Islam has never been the monopoly of one particular race or nation. When we look at the map of the modern world we find that the great majority of Muslims are not Arabs, the racial community into which Muhammad happened to have been born. Eighty-five percent of his community are of other stock, including Turks, Africans, Indonesians and six million Europeans. And never has there been any consciousness of race in Islam, for the Qur'an teaches that all are one family, and that "the most noble in God's sight is he who fears Him most;" likewise, the Blessed Prophet affirmed that "there shall be no distinction between white and black". From Siberia to central Africa traditional Islamic societies have taken root and have flourished, demonstrating the workability of the Islamic system in a complex variety of milieux.

As for that phenomenon questionably termed "progress", it has never impaired Islam's relevance and effectiveness. Islam, as the Prophet taught it, works well in the technological age; indeed, it seems to be the only religion which has retained its dynamism and character intact in the modern world. There has never been any confrontation between science and revelation in the Muslim context, for the Qur'an is remarkably free of the inaccuracies regarding the natural world which some other scriptures are said to contain. Islam functions in a Harlem ghetto as well as it does in a Bengali village: culturally it differs, for Islam is not a culture, but is rather a force which conditions cultures, but what is happening is still recognisably Islam, doctrinally and socially respecting its parameters.

God spared Islam the agonies of fossilisation and diminishing meaning, ensuring its universal applicability in a changing world. Earlier faiths fell victim to clerisy, whose representatives sanctified tyranny and iniquity. Islam was forbidden to create a priestly class. Rather, it developed a tradition of religious scholars, the *ulema*, who, although they were possessed of no special sacramental function, nevertheless provided the intellectual rearticulation of eternal truth to a world in constant flux. It was the *ulema* who assessed new legal situations, new doctrinal challenges, and who suggested ways in which an adaptation to novel circumstances could be effected while remaining loyal to the revelation of the Qur'an and the teachings of the Prophet. This process of adaptation is termed *Ijtihad*, a technical and highly sophisticated science of jurisprudence which, while affirming the timeless efficacy of the social teachings set down in revelation, provides a means for the systematic extension of these guidelines when circumstances demand. Thus Islam today is still practiced as it was in the time of the Blessed Prophet, constituting a living chain of transmission with the past, thereby retaining its original freshness and simplicity, but able to face the challenges and complexities of the age with new, yet authentically Muslim rulings regarding such twentieth-century marvels as nuclear weapons and surrogate motherhood.

This capacity, not for change, but for expansion, undoubtedly constitutes a key factor in Islam's continuing dynamism. As Bernard Shaw remarked, "I have always held the religion of Mohammed in high esteem because of its wonderful vitality. To me it seems the only faith able to adapt to life under different conditions in a way which makes it attractive to every people and every age." For other faiths, busily reforming themselves to such a degree that they would be unrecognisable to the faithful of an earlier generation, have thereby lost confidence in those spiritual and ethical teachings which by their very nature challenge the world, and may not be challenged; which transform, and are not transformed.

Chapter Two

Revelation and the Unseen

The Qur'an: Literally, 'that which is often recited'. A web of rhythm and meaning, the words of which throb through Muslim worship and which at every point in the believer's life break surface, sanctifying existence with the scent of eternity. A paradoxical flash of the divine light, penetrating the veil of solid existence into our world. Redolent with symbol, half-hidden meaning and rapier-sharp insight, it transforms the reader by suggestion rather than by formal structures of argument and proof. It demands to be accepted on its own terms: only when the reader is prepared to discard all that he believes a book should be will he begin to discern its symmetries and its heartrending power.

Goethe sensed this. In his *West-Oestlicher Divan* he declares how, after inspiring initial astonishment and fear, the Qur'an "soon attracts, astounds, and, in the end, enforces our reverence. Its style, in accordance with its contents and aim, is stern, grand, terrible – ever and anon truly sublime. Thus, this book will go on exercising, through the ages, a most potent influence."

And so it does: more so for the Muslim than for the most committed Protestant, holy writ is studied, memorised and quoted. More than four million men and women in the world today have memorised the entire Qur'an: over six thousand verses. A far greater number have memorised shorter sections for use in their five daily prayers. And throughout the Muslim world, from Senegal to Indonesia, to ride any bus or train is to see one's fellow-passengers quietly reading from a miniature copy of God's Book, or reciting it to themselves, enjoying a breath of the transcendent to relieve the tedium of their journey. The same Book, in intricate calligraphy, adorns the rear window of passing cars. Short, aphoristic verses are painted on the walls and doors of houses. The conversation of city businessman and rustic peasant alike is peppered with allusions and direct quotations from the Book. Everywhere human life is anchored to the hidden world by the Qur'an.

For the Muslim, God's Book is much more than a source of liturgical and social rules; indeed, such topics occupy less than one tenth of the Qur'anic text; and it is more even than a revelatory declaration of man's origin and his fate, an exposition of the truths of man's spiritual nature and of judgement. The Qur'an is 'oft-recited', at the most profound possible level, because it is of God. Its text reveals God's will for His creation, but is also a revelation of Himself. It is uncreated, timeless, a dimension of God's pre-existent attribute of speech, communication: it is the Logos, which is the interface between the Absolute and the contingent realms. It is the pre-existent light which becomes manifest in history as prophethood.

With the advent of Muhammad – may God bless him and grant him peace – the Qur'an was revealed as a Book for the first time in its entirety. Previous revelations offer to us brief flashes from certain facets of the *Umm-al-Kitab*, the "Mother of the Book", which later became known to mankind as the Qur'an, but the fullest manifestation waited until the final, eschatological dispensation of Islam. Hence the Prophetic nature of the figure of Muhammad, his light, was not other than the Qur'an. As his wife A'isha expressed it: "He was the Qur'an walking."

Thus it is that in the Muslim devotional life the Book is so often associated with the Prophet. "Truly, God and his Angels invoke blessings upon the Prophet" the sacred text runs. "O you who believe, invoke salutations and blessings upon him!" This act of benediction is called the Prayer on the Prophet, and forms a spiritual bridge for man, who by praying for the Prophet comes into contact with God's outpourings of blessings and knowledge which is mediated through his person, the receptacle of the Qur'an.

This intermediary role of the Book has deep implications for the way in which the text is perceived. Merely to pronounce one word of it is to participate in the energy which underlay Prophethood, even if the reader is not capable of putting it to use more than fractionally. Even the ordering of the text follows its patterns of spiritual meaning. This is why Islamic art has traditionally paid so much attention to the decoration, calligraphy and binding of the sacred Book of Islam: formally and spiritually, and also aesthetically, the Book lies at the very reverential core of Muslim life.

The text itself was revealed in sections to the Prophet. As the infant Muslim community grew in understanding and strength new depth was constantly being added to its insight by new episodes of revelation. But this progression is little evidenced by the text in its final form, as it was approved by the Prophet before his death. The reader finds the Book prefaced with a chapter of relatively late revelation, the "Chapter of the Opening":

> In the name of God, the Compassionate, the
> > Merciful.
> Praise be to God, the Lord of the Worlds,
> The Compassionate, the Merciful,
> King of Judgement-day!
> You alone do we worship, and to You alone do we
> > turn for help.
> Guide us in the straight Path;
> The Path of those whom You have favoured; not of
> > those with whom You are angered, nor of
> > those who go astray.

This Chapter is followed by another of much greater length, then the remainder of the Book unfolds in Chapters which become progressively more succinct. On this great canvas are set, together with the necessary guidelines for law and liturgy, the tremendous questions which have ever exercised mankind, cast in longer or shorter leitmotivs which outline the life stories of earlier Prophets, interweaved with exhortations to read the signs which have been carved into nature and history.

A characteristic text is the following:

> So glory be to God,
> in your evening hour
> and in your morning hour.
> His is the praise

in the heavens and the earth,
at the setting of the sun,
and at your noontide hour.
He brings forth the living from the dead, and brings
   forth the dead from the living, and gives
   life to the earth after its death; Thus shall
   be the Resurrection.

And it is of His signs
that He created you of dust, then you are people,
   scattered about.

And it is of His signs
that He created for you, of yourselves, spouses, that
   you might find tranquillity in them, and
   He has set between you love and mercy.
   Surely in this are signs for people who
   consider.

And of His signs
is the creation of the heavens and the earth, and the
   variety of your tongues and hues; surely
   in this are signs for those who know.
   (XXX, 18-22)

The following early verses were addressed to the
Prophet himself:

In the name of God, the Compassionate, the
   Merciful.
By the morning hours,
and the night when it broods;
your Lord has not forsaken you or hated you,
and the afterlife shall be better for you than the
   former life.

Your Lord shall give to you, and you shall
          be well-pleased.
Did He not find you an orphan, and shelter you?
Did He not find you erring, and guide you?
Did He not find you needy, and suffice you?
As for the orphan, be not harsh to him,
As for the beggar, scold him not;
and as for your Lord's blessing, declare it!
          (XCIII, 1-12)

The story of the Annunciation is told in especially moving words:

And mention in the Book, Mary
when she retired from her people to an eastern
          place.
And she took a veil apart from them;
then We sent unto her Our spirit
that appeared to her as a man without fault.
She said, "I take refuge in the All-Merciful from
          you.
If you fear God . . ."
He said, "I am but a messenger come from your
          Lord, to bestow upon you a boy most pure."
She said, "How shall I have a son, whom no man
          has touched, neither have I been
          unchaste?"
He said, "Even so your Lord has said:
'Easy is that for Me, and that We may appoint him
          a sign unto men and a mercy from Us; it is
          a thing decreed'."
So she conceived him, and withdrew with him to a
          distant place . . .
          (XIX, 16-22)

One of the best known verses, ever a subject for mystical contemplation, is the so-called Verse of Light:

> God is the Light of the heavens and the earth; the likeness of His Light is as a niche wherein is a lamp. The lamp is in a glass, the glass is as it were a shining star, kindled from a blessed tree, an olive, neither of the East nor of the West. Its oil would well-nigh shine, even if no fire touched it. Light upon Light; God guides to His Light whom He will. And God strikes similitudes for men, and God has knowledge of all things.

(XXIV, 35)

One of the most surprising features of the Qur'an to the Western reader coming to it for the first time is the way in which subjects of many kinds may be found together in a single chapter, or even in the course of a few verses. This is an essential aspect of the Book's message. It is human nature to endeavour to categorise and label our experience of the world, and we feel disconcerted when our familiar expectations of such an ordering are not fulfilled. The Qur'an, both in its literary style and in its internal arrangement, conforms to no human norms. It is a message which has broken through the veil of the unseen, and causes us to look upwards, bringing us suddenly into a new dimension, a new mode of perception. The Qur'an is from the One, and it belongs to a higher order of creation than our own, where unity and differentiation begin to coalesce, and where our perception of a world dispersed into multiple states and forms loses its validity. But despite this unique feature, the formal message, the outward meaning of the Book is in no way compromised; indeed, it gains in cogency, for each of its teachings and guiding principles is meaningful only in the context of the transcendent unity of God.

The question of the sequence of topics found in the Qur'an blends into another issue: the miraculous quality of the Book's semantics and diction. For Muslims it is an article of faith that the prose style with which its meaning patterns are articulated is inimitable in its beauty, precision and moving grandeur, and that this constitutes the greatest of the miracles with which God confirmed the message of His last Prophet. This quality, known in Arabic as the i'jaz, comes over only very imperfectly even in the best translations; nevertheless it is still possible for the European reader to sense something of the breathless, insistent rhythms of the original. To the Arab, whether Muslim or Christian, the Qur'an has always remained the summit of eloquence which every stylist should aspire to emulate. Perhaps the greatest of all the arts evolved by Islamic civilisation is that of the formal, virtuoso recitation of the Book before an audience, which is frequently moved to tears by the majestic cadences of a favourite Chapter, faithfully rendered by some master-craftsman of the human voice.

So important is the i'jaz as a feature of the Qur'an that past translators, whatever their own religious commitments, have not failed to draw attention to the magnetic force of the Book's language. The first great rendition into English of the Muslim scripture was the work of the eighteenth century orientalist

George Sale. In his Preliminary Discourse he tells us:

> And to this miracle Mohammad himself chiefly appealed for the confirmation of his mission, publicly challenging the most eloquent men in Arabia, which was at the same time stocked with thousands whose sole study and ambition it was to excel in elegance of style and composition, to produce even a single chapter that might be compared with it. I will mention but one instance out of several, to show that this Book was really admired for the beauty of its composition by those who must be allowed to have been competent judges. A poem of Labid Ebn Rabia, in Mohammad's time, being affixed to the gate of the temple in Mecca, an honour allowed to none but the most esteemed performances, none of the other poets dared offer anything of their own in competition with it. But the second Chapter of the Koran being affixed near it soon after, Labid himself (then an idolater) on reading the first verse only, was struck with admiration, and immediately professed the religion taught therein, declaring that such words could proceed from an inspired person only.

It is part of the timeless efficacy of *i'jaz* that whenever Islam makes headway in some new environment it is the directness and power of the Qur'an's language that moves people to seek entrance into its world. The former rock star Cat Stevens set his faith in Islam solely on the basis of reading a copy that he had received as a gift from his brother. In the same spirit, in 1982, the former deputy speaker of the French parliament, the philosopher and literary critic Roger Garaudy also embraced Islam after a lifetime's fascination with the beauty and vigour of its scriptures.

The Qur'an, then, is for the Muslim believer the greatest of the signs of God in the material world. Although readable and rapidly intelligible, it possesses features which clearly mark it as belonging to another kingdom lying beyond human perceptions. Its teachings have proved all-embracing, and have provided the foundations for great civilisations. Its text has defied all attempts at imitation. As a bridge to God it has retained its every efficacy, uncorrupted by interpolation or tendentious exegesis, as every historian confesses, providing a metaphysical *cantus firmus* in the lives of countless millions throughout history and into the present day.

The Qur'an was revealed through the Angel of Revelation Gabriel. Over a period of twenty-three years the Blessed Prophet would receive the visits of the Angel, when a portion of the Book would be revealed to him. Upon the Prophet's death the Angel declared that never again would he appear to man. But there are other messengers and servants of God in the angelic realm, some of whom we must one day meet. The Qur'an and the teachings of the Prophet speak of a number of Angels, who belong to a world not normally accessible to human senses. They are created of light, and are hence subtle and non-solid. We are told of six in particular: Gabriel, the Angel of Revelation; Mikael, who brings God's prosperity and bounty to man; Israfil, responsible for blowing the Last Trump; Azrael, the Angel of Death, who takes man's soul when his lifespan ends; Malek, the Angel supervising hell; and finally, Radwan, who is responsible for Paradise.

In addition to these, mention should be made of two Angels whom we shall encounter shortly after death. These are Munkar and Nakir, who question the newly-dead regarding their lives and beliefs.

The Angels, as we have said, are creatures of light. They are created incapable of rebellion against God's will, for their purpose is to carry it out. This is why Islam sees man as potentially superior to the Angels, for he may freely choose to serve God and to believe in His Prophets, whereas the Angels, who are at all times in the presence of God, cannot fail to obey Him and to sing His praises at all times. By the same token, man can be lower than the Angels, and lower even than the animals, should he choose not to worship his Creator and thank Him for the gift of life and the blessings showered upon him in this world and, we are given to hope, the next.

It is in this sense that we are to understand the story of Adam's repentance, told at the very beginning of the Qur'an. God commanded the Angels to bow down to Adam after He had created him. One refused, failing to recognise the potential superiority of man, and was cast out from God's presence to be His instrument of misguidance. This creature is traditionally called in the English language Satan, who ever since his fall has been working to lead man into self-adoration rather than the worship of his Creator.

Clearly the Qur'anic picture of the angelic world differs from that which is familiar to Westerners. European legend has created an elaborate science of angelology, as artists such as Masaccio and Botticelli gave full vent to their imagination in depicting essentially human figures sprouting wings of various shapes and degrees of improbability. When the Book of Islam speaks of Angels it is clearly reaffirming a principle of creation known to all other divine religions, but nowhere does it state that they must always assume a specific form. Only in the story of the Annunciation does Gabriel appears as "a fair man".

So far we have investigated the nature of Muslim revelation and of the angelic hierarchy whose existence it affirms and through which it was mediated to the realm of space and time. Yet one element is still missing. Although we have said something of the nature of the Prophet as the vessel of the pre-existent Qur'an, we have paid little attention to the material circumstances surrounding his life and mission. The Qur'anic event is not separable from the life of the Prophet to whom it was entrusted. "He was the Qur'an walking," his wife said, and it is only through a close and reverent familiarity with the moving tale of his life that its greatest secrets are divulged.

We are fortunate to have at our disposal a wealth of historical material relating to the career of the Prophet of Islam. The consistency and contemporary nature of the early chronicles means that we have a far clearer and more detailed picture of his life than we can claim to possess with regard to the founders of most other religions and schools of thought. The Qur'an itself, the textual integrity of which remains unimpeached, constitutes a rich mine of information relating to the circumstances in which it made its appearance. The incidents and major events of the Prophet's life are recounted with such consistency and by such a wide variety of historical accounts that the historicity of the traditional picture of his achievement is not in doubt to modern scholarship.

Muhammad, whose name means "the praise-worthy", was born at Mecca in the year 570 AD. By the time he reached the age of six both his parents were dead, and he was placed in the care of his uncle Abu Talib. Abu Talib was a successful merchant who regularly travelled to the great cities of Syria which lay to the north, and it was during the course of one of these journeys that the first indication of the unusual status of his nephew appeared. The young Muhammad was twelve years of age when his uncle first agreed to let him accompany him to Syria. After many weeks they arrived at the well of Bostra, the scene of the first miracle of Islam. At Bostra there lived a Christian hermit by the name of Bahira. Upon catching a glimpse of the future Prophet he told Abu Talib: "Return with this boy and guard him well, for a great career awaits him."

But for the next thirty years Muhammad lived an uneventful life as a merchant, acquiring a reputation for scrupulous honesty in all his dealings. The only cause for people's curiosity was his periodic trips to a neighbouring mountain, where he would spend days on end in meditation. He could feel no affinity with the beliefs of his fellow-countrymen, immersed as they were in the most primitive superstition and idolatry, neither could he find satisfaction in the myriad versions of Christianity. It was during one of these periods of quiet seclusion, far from the distractions of the world, that he received the first revelation.

The Angel Gabriel appeared before him, and seizing hold of him, said: "Read!" "I cannot," replied the Prophet. "Read!" the Angel demanded again. And again the Prophet replied: "I cannot!" A third time the Angel repeated his command, and then added, "Read, in the name of thy Lord, Who created; created man from a clot of blood. Read, for thy Lord is the most Generous, Who taught the use of the pen, Who taught man that which he did not know."

These words constituted the first text of the Qur'an to be revealed. The rest came progressively through the remainder of the Prophet's life, speaking each time to a larger audience. The first to believe in the truth of his mission was his wife, who was followed in her faith by a small but growing band of followers, who braved the mockery and violence of the townspeople of Mecca, and who persevered in the face of the most cruel persecution and torture. The great men of the city came to the Prophet offering to withdraw their opposition to him and his followers if he would only renounce his religion, or at the very least recognise their gods, yet he steadfastly declined, declaring that the one God Who had conferred the degree of Prophethood upon him could allow no man or idol to be worshipped besides Him. Astonished, but finally convinced of his sincerity, the Meccan elders left him, but continued their persecutions and killings with renewed ferocity.

The revelation, however, continued. Even the Arabs who refused to abjure their idols were bewildered and humbled by the soaring eloquence of its diction and by its capacity to relate tales of the ancient prophets of whom they had often never heard. They were particularly puzzled by the Book's insistence on the reality of judgement and life after death, a notion wholly unfamiliar to their traditional understanding of the world. Slowly, impressed by both the remarkable nature of the Book and by the saintly conduct of the Prophet himself, who maintained his tradition of generosity and charity in the face of the most cruel adversity, individual men and women came to him secretly to be admitted to the religion which he taught.

During the twelfth year of his mission, the faith of his little community received its critical test. One night, the Prophet was transported bodily from the Sacred Place of Worship at Mecca to the Temple Mount of Jerusalem. Today a golden dome, the most famous landmark of the Celestial City, stands over the rock from which he was then taken, in the company of the Angels, into the presence of God. During this ascent, celebrated today throughout the Muslim world as the feast of the *Isra' wa'l-Mi'raj*, he met with many of the Prophets who had preceded him, including Moses and Jesus. And when Gabriel came finally with him to a point closer to God than had been attained by any previous Prophet, the Angel stopped, and told him: "Were I to proceed further I would be burnt." The Prophet Muhammad, however, uniquely honoured by his Lord, continued to that point described in the Qur'anic account as the "Lote-tree of the Boundary", a vivid symbol of the point where the multiplicity of existence branches out from the level of complete Unity.

This experience constituted in many ways the culmination of Prophethood. And while in the Presence of his Lord the Prophet was given to instruct his companions to observe the five daily prayers, which themselves are symbols of the experience given to the Prophet at Jerusalem. As the Prophet said: "The Prayer is the Ascension (*mi'raj*) of the believer."

In the same year, the situation began to improve for the Muslim community. Not at Mecca – for by now the Muslims were obliged to live in an outlying district, effectively ostracised by their countrymen – but abroad. Twelve men of the northern city of Yathrib who were visiting Mecca on business embraced Islam, and, despite the hazards involved, undertook to spread it in their native city upon their return. The following year a delegation of seventy-five Muslims arrived from Yathrib, and seeing the precarious situation of the group around the Prophet, invited them to return with them to their own city.

The Muslims were quick to agree. Over the next few months companies of men and women made their way quietly out of Mecca and began the lengthy and difficult road to their new haven. The last to leave was the Prophet himself, accompanied by his closest companion, Abu Bakr. Thus was completed the *hijra*, the emigration of the Prophet, which forms today the starting-point of the Muslim calendar.

Once settled at Yathrib, which soon came to be known as *al-Madina al-Munawwara*, the Illuminated City, the Muslim community grew rapidly in numbers. For the first time they were able to call people to their religion without fear of reprisal, and could establish a place of worship for themselves.

The elders of Mecca, infuriated that the Prophet had slipped away from them, lost no time in preparing a military expedition to crush Islam and hopefully to capture its Prophet. An army of a thousand men approached Medina and began to uproot crops and to steal livestock. Upon seeing this, the Prophet issued a call to arms. A small detachment of approximately three hundred Muslims set out to meet the Meccan host. The two forces met by the wells of Badr, and soon it became clear that the Muslims, despite their inferior numbers, were winning the day. The Meccans fled, leaving a number of their champions dead on the battlefield, and Medina was safe until the following year.

Although the next battle, which took place near the mountain of Uhud, ended in defeat for the Muslims, the Meccans failed to press home their advantage, and were content to return to their city. There then followed a period of peace, in which the Muslim community grew in numbers, and during which the characteristic features of its society took shape. Medina became transformed into a political entity under the direction of the Prophet, ruled by the laws of the Qur'an. This inaugurated a golden age of toleration and brotherhood, as the barbarous social forms that had characterised pre-Islamic Arabia were swept away, to be replaced by the principle of the commonalty of mankind under God.

By the time six years had passed since the Emigration from Mecca, the Muslims felt themselves strong enough to dare to undertake the great Pilgrimage to Mecca, that ancient institution commemorating Abraham's sojourn there, when he laid the foundations of the Ka'ba, the empty cube which was the first place of worship built by mankind. The Prophet, accompanied by approximately eight hundred of his followers, all totally unarmed, set out for Mecca. When they reached its vicinity, at a place known as al-Hudaybiyya, they were confronted by an army of idolators from the city, and were forced to give up their plan of visiting the Sacred Prencincts that year. But they concluded a treaty with the Meccan representatives in which it was agreed that a cessation of hostilities was to be observed for ten years.

The treaty of al-Hudaybiyya, however, was destined to be broken before two years had passed. A tribe loyal to Mecca launched an attack on the tribe of Khuza'a, who were in allegiance with the Muslims. Thus the Prophet ordered that the Muslim army was to march on Mecca to demand an explanation. Upon arrival with ten thousand men he entered the city, which at first seemed quite deserted. Then it became apparent that the townspeople had locked themselves into their homes out of fright, anticipating a massacre. Their astonishment could hardly have been greater when the Prophet announced a general amnesty, proclaiming that everyone who had participated in the war against his cause, and who had tortured his companions during the difficult days when Islam was persecuted and harried from every side, was to be forgiven.

This great act of mercy, when coupled with the sight of their idols being torn down and destroyed, moved the hearts of the people of Mecca, and soon, after hearing the teachings of the Prophet expounded to them, they had for the most part joined Islam. Messengers were despatched far and wide, to Persia, Egypt and Byzantium, carrying with them news of the Prophet's mission. Throughout Arabia, and further afield still, men and women of all backgrounds learnt of the new Prophet and put their faith in his teachings. Throughout the ancient world individuals and communities embraced Islam, often in the face of terrible persecution, and the blazingly simple truth of the Unity of God took root once more, displacing, but never with violence, the Christian sects.

By the tenth year of the Muslim calendar deputations from all over Arabia and beyond had come to meet the Prophet of Islam and to pledge the allegiance of their people to his cause. Expecting to find a wealthy king, they were amazed to be shown into the presence of a gentle and humble man in patched but spotlessly clean robes, who wore a quiet smile, and who commanded the evident devotion and love of his followers. Rather than finding a palace, they were taken to a small hut close by the mosque, where the Prophet lived in conditions of great modesty. And they found a land of light, full of worship, generosity and saintliness, which described itself simply as *Dar al-Islam*, the abode of Islam – a world of peaceful surrender to God.

The Hindu philosopher Rajakrishna sums up his personality thus:

> Muhammad was a sovereign to whom all his domains bowéd down in wilfull submission, yet he was extremely humble. He considered himself as possessing nothing, for everything was in the hands of his Lord. We find

43

him in boundless wealth; the coffers of his treasury used to be filled from the wealth of his territories, yet he always remained in want. His house remained without food for days and he very often went to sleep without food and continued fasting the next day. We find him as an excellent commander leading a small force against huge armies well-equipped with arms and ammunition and yet inflicting heavy losses and defeat against such huge numbers. We find him as a valiant hero standing alone against the thousands of those opposing him. Yet he was kindhearted and had an aversion to bloodshed. He was concerned with the affairs of the whole Arabian peninsula, yet he did not fail to look after the minutest details of his own household, besides catering for the Muslims, particularly the poor and indigent among them.

He was somebody who was concerned with the whole world, yet was devoted to meditation and worship; thus, he was in the world and yet far from it, for he was always seeking the pleasure of God. He did not know how to take revenge for the sake of revenge, and he used to pray for the good of all, even his enemy. He was very rational and unfaltering even when he was hailed as the triumphant conqueror of nations. He used to live a very humble life with his family, sleeping on straw mats and suffering from all kind of needs at a time when booty was flowing in from all parts. All such booty he used to distribute among the poor.

In the eleventh year of the Hijra the Prophet died in the arms of his devoted wife A'isha. Despite initial consternation and grief the course he had mapped out was pursued; revelation had come to an end and his religion now stood in its completed form, but the great task of spreading its principles of forgiveness and peace in a troubled world still lay ahead. The achievements of his companions and their successors constitute an almost unrivalled chapter in the history of the rise of civilisations. A century on from his death, a new sacred civilisation was flourishing from the Pyrenees to the Indus, unified under one ruler, the caliph, and enjoying the full prosperity and tolerance guaranteed it by God's law. The population of the ancient world soared, cities were rebuilt, and great literature and architecture once again appeared.

The mission of a Prophet, by the good providence of God, had succeeded.

Chapter Three

The Muslim Life

The definitive attribute of man is his ability to forget. The very word used in the Qur'an for "man", *insaan*, is related etymologically to the word *nisiaan*, or forgetfulness. Created not, as in Christianity, in a state of some "original sin", but rather in a condition of grace, the human creature progressively loses his awareness of the immediate presence of God as he is initiated into the world.

It is the function of religion to make us remember. Through its two great halves, doctrine and practice, which in Islam are enshrined in the dual testimony of faith, it serves to remind a distracted humanity of who and where we are ("doctrine"), and how we may confirm and strengthen this knowledge in the way we live ("practice": liturgy, ethics, and law). This process of reminding acknowledges the presence of a fundamental mystery which has been built into the very warp and woof of creation: the paradox of free will.

Modern science has reduced the natural world to a field of matter, which may equally well be seen as a field of energy. Chaos prevails at this most elemental level of the system, while order – baffling to the atheist – appears at the molecular level, climaxing in the intricate achievements of human art and thought. At each moment, every particle in this higher system is bound by the immutable laws of physics. In religious language: all things move in submission to God's ordering of His creation. Into this flawless, elaborate system He has set man, His viceroy. Now, although man's physical elements are in themselves intrinsically bound to obey the inexorable laws of creation, he is set apart in having been endowed with a soul, which is in its innermost core not of this world, but of God.

Thus the atheist (and particularly the Marxist) tends inescapably towards fatalism, believing that all he does and will do has been preordained by the laws of science. Only the man of faith can truly claim something which, however circumscribed, is still free will. For the laws of the creation can be overturned if the Lawmaker so desires. The Muslim, recognising that to be human is to be the channel of transcendent intervention in the running of the world's mechanisms, is thus set free from determinism and fatalism, for he alone knows of the possibility of miracle, which signifies nothing other than the overturning of physical laws.

The believer sees the hand of God in all things, but he knows, nonetheless, that by virtue of humanity's central and deputative position in the cosmos God may also allow him, in addition to the enjoyment of the beauty and joys of the world, to strive to improve both his own life and a world badly corrupted by the ignorant, by virtue of his status as his Lord's "vicegerent". This realisation, that we are empowered, as responsible trustees, to do with the universe as we see fit, must inspire in us a profound and abiding sense of gratitude. This gratitude must be the dominant emotion in the lives of the men and women who recognise God's love and honouring of them through the gifts, material and spiritual, which He has conferred upon them. Gratitude, in its higher and purer reaches turns into praise; in other words, the focus shifts from man's thanking God to God's being thanked by man. A new flux is set up in the cosmos: God's outpouring to man in the form of His gifts and the ability to use them, now counterpoints man's corresponding praise of his Maker.

But this "praise" is not easy. However strong the motivation behind it may be, it is hard for us to express ourselves in a manner worthy of addressing the First Cause. Just as when an ordinary man addresses an aristocrat he expresses his respect most fully by using a certain protocol, so when we turn to God we must find some way of presenting what we feel in a way befitting the presence of the Lord of creation, Who has given us all we possess.

This protocol we call "worship". While we may find many ways of worship which afford us some satisfaction, the finest and most devotional forms cannot be dreamed up by man, and are best granted directly by God. Worship is a complex and subtle activity, relying heavily on symbolism; a complete science, in fact, involving not only a profound understanding of the human mind, but also a direct knowledge of the kingdom of God. The Qur'an provides a complete and deeply satisfying system of worship: simple, dignified, yet profoundly moving and transformative. But although in the Islamic vision all human activity must be a form of worship, four specific forms of devotion are laid down and particularly emphasised. Chief among these is the regular prayer, followed by the month of fasting, and the similarly purifying experiences of systematic almsgiving and the great Pilgrimage to the sacred precincts at Mecca. These 'pillars of Islam' are obligatory for every believer, whether man or woman (for, contrary to the belief of most outsiders, who learn of Islam from newspapers rather than from theological works, men and women are regarded by the classical Muslim authorities as being equal in God's sight).

Prayer, in Arabic *salat*, is very much in evidence to the visitor to a Muslim community. Not just in the overflowing mosques but seemingly in each corner and crevice of every building, men and women stand and bow towards the Holy City. The taxi driver halts during a slack hour, and unrolls a small intricate carpet, and prays by the busy roadside. The employees in some provincial town hall leave their desks during their lunch break to eat and also to pray. Hearing the Call to Prayer from a distant mosque, farmworkers lay down their tools, and humbly face Mecca on pieces of cardboard or rush matting.

Five times in every day the Muslim turns his back on whatever has been preoccupying him, and bows and prostrates in abject submission before his Creator. In ten minutes' time he will be back at work, but with an evident burden lifted and a new expression on his face. For the regular act of *salat* is a powerful aid to the constant, unceasing remembrance of the eternal presence of God. Islam forbade monasteries: it never needed them. Man is not to shut himself up away from the world, rendering his service to God a purely selfish activity; rather he must be a participant in the joys and sorrows of the world, which for those who understand is an arena for self-discipline and austerity more effective than any monk's cell. Through the prayer he constantly pulls himself back to the remembrance of God and acquires the ability to see the hand of the Lord in everything which befalls him. The Prophet Muhammad once compared it to a stream running by a house. "If a man were to wash in the stream," he said, "five times a day, would any dirt remain on his body?" "None," replied his companions. And he remarked, "So it is with the five Prayers, with which God wipes away all faults."

These five daily acts of devotion, which are said at dawn, noon, midafternoon, sunset and in the evening, are best prayed in the company of others. But the Qur'an teaches that for those who wish, other prayers are particularly effective when observed at other times also. In particular the Prophet used to spend long hours before dawn in prayer before his Lord, so much so that his wife A'isha once complained about this, saying: "Why should you spend so much time in prayer when the creation is asleep, when God has forgiven you all your transgressions?" And the Prophet replied simply: "O A'isha, am I not to be a grateful servant?"

Each of the prayers is announced vocally in the Call to Prayer, or *adhan*. The "muezzin", who may be anyone from the local community, stands in an elevated place, usually the tall graceful tower known as a minaret, and sings forth the following declaration:

> *God is Most Great, God is Most Great.*
> *God is Most Great, God is Most Great.*
> *I testify that there is no deity save God.*

I testify that there is no deity save God.
I testify that Muhammad is the Messenger of God.
I testify that Muhammad is the Messenger of God.
Come to the Prayer, Come to the Prayer;
Come to success, Come to success.
God is Most Great, God is Most Great.
There is no deity save God.

In its directness and stark simplicity the call evokes an instant response in those that hear it. For to them it serves as a reminder that through their daily existence, with its hopes and its disappointments, there runs a thread of Divine remembrance which calls them to make their every act affirm the unity and omnipresent nature of God. And at the Dawn Call, sent forth just as light is beginning to show on the horizon, the muezzin adds: "Prayer is better than sleep! Prayer is better than sleep!" to rouse us from our lazy slumber to stand before our Creator at that blessed hour, thanking Him for our lives and the good things of His providing, and asking Him for fuller participation in His light, and for forgiveness and joy on the Day of Judgement.

After the call for each of these prayers is delivered there are a few minutes during which people make their way to the mosque and offer certain optional prayers before the congregational worship is begun.

Mosque buildings vary enormously in shape and scope, another manifestation of the cultural richness and diversity of Islam. But in each one it is necessary to remove one's shoes at the door. This makes for cleanliness, and also assures a quietness and gentleness inside the prayer hall. There is no furniture, but usually the floor is covered with rich carpets. There are no statues or human representations, or any symbolic depiction of any kind, for such would only serve as a distraction; instead the recurrent motif of the arabesque leads the eye through geometric devices and patterns which suggest the intricate consistency of God's creation. A niche let into one wall indicates the direction of prayer. As was once the case in Christian churches, there are separate sections for men and women, to avoid the natural possibility of distraction, however slight, during the course of worship.

The mosque is open at all times, and not just for the five prayers. Constantly people are to be seen coming and going, praying individually, reciting the Qur'an, or just sitting down for a while to rest and absorb the tranquillity of the place. In addition, the mosque, as the social hub of the neighbourhood, traditionally provides free education for children, and also, and particularly in this century, a health clinic funded by local donations and staffed by volunteers.

Having made his ablutions and arrived at the mosque the worshipper walks over to where the congregation is gathering. After all who are present have finished their preparatory optional prayers one man steps forward. This is the Imam, whose function it is to ensure the straightness of the rows of worshippers, and who leads the prayer, coordinating thereby the movements of those behind him, who may be two or three, or several thousand. As we have said, he is not a priest, but only the member of the congregation generally thought to be the most learned and devout, and who is chosen by the general consensus of those present.

The Imam stands before the first row with his back to the worshippers, and the second call to prayer, known as the *iqama*, is delivered, which announces to all present the imminent beginning of the prayer. The Imam then recalls God in his heart, and raising his hands to the sides of his head, says in a voice imbued with awe and humility, *Allahu Akbar*: "God is Most Great", thus affirming the insignificance of all that had been busying him before the prayer began. The assembled ranks behind him do likewise, then all place their hands on their chests, right over left. The Imam then recites the Opening Chapter of the Qur'an, followed by another passage of his choosing. During the noon and midafternoon prayers, however, the recitation is done in silence.

Then the Imam calls *Allahu Akbar* once more, and the men and women behind him bow in submission to their Creator. After standing once more the worshippers prostate together, assuming the position of the utmost humility and adoration. Each worshipper whispers quietly to himself, "Glory to my Lord, the Most High", thereby affirming God's power and exaltation while in a position of the most complete surrender and abasement. As the Prophet said: "Man is closest to his Lord when he prostrates".

Within ten minutes the prayer has drawn to a close. It is usually followed by a number of short litanies chosen and recited by each worshipper as he feels appropriate. Often hands are raised in supplication, asking the Lord in devotion and sincerity to grant His love and mercy, or petitioning Him for some secret need.

A few more individual prayers are said, and then people begin to leave the mosque, transformed by this sudden change of direction and restored to a fuller and more natural awareness of God. They return to their work with vigour and a new energy, having been calmed and spiritually recharged by the experience of facing their Creator.

As the years pass and the discipline of regular worship begins to take effect, certain profound changes begin to come over those who maintain it. For each time they are "cleansing themselves with the water of heaven". If they understand their worship correctly and allow it to purify the interstices of their lives which lie between the prayers, then each new act of devotion will not merely restore what has been lost, but will provide a step upwards on the ladder of spiritual growth. Every prayer will become more and more absorbing, more and more powerful and awesome, until our whole lives become infused with the awareness of God's grace and protection. By the same token, every moment in which we are not at prayer will become a form of prayer itself, and we will find that in our spare time nothing seems so fulfilling and moving as facing God anew, declaring His name in humility and wonder. The world in which we live will thus change in meaning for us, from being a space of taking and profit into being a realm of pure service to God and to our fellow men, for as our spiritual horizons widen we will learn to take delight in selflessness.

It is thus that a reply can be made to the question of why prayers should be observed at fixed times rather than whenever the moment seems appropriate. It hardly needs saying that whenever one wishes to pray one should do so, exploiting the opportunity and the inclination to the fullest. Yet it would seem equally clear that to pray only when one is in the right mood is far from sufficient. In fact, the time when we least feel like praying is often when we need it most. To obey God by observing the five prayers He has laid down for us ensures that we will remember Him in times both of ease and of difficulty, and that there will never be a period of more than a few hours in which we do not turn to God. Obedience and submission are a far stronger basis for spiritual growth than part-time or random religiosity.

This discipline demands in its beginning stages an ability to concentrate. The outward forms of worship are of great assistance in bringing about a prayerful environment and state of mind, but they cannot guarantee that the worshipper will be thinking about God and not about his next meal. To begin with, prayer requires of us firm and directed thinking, and constant concentration. As time goes by, however, this effort yields its rewards. The Muslim finds himself to be more and more absorbed in the prayer, until any thought of material affairs seems banal and insipid beside the pleasure of holding conversation with God. When this emotion prevails, he will want to "give life to the night," as the Blessed Prophet put it, by praying for several hours at the silent time before dawn.

There is one more aspect of the Muslim prayer which we should mention. In the vision of the Qur'an, prayer has a social impact. As God says: "Prayer distances us from evil, corruption and aggressiveness." The mechanism of this is complex, but it is nevertheless clear that as the inward voyage progresses, the one engaged upon it finds himself simultaneously drawn both into and away from the society which surrounds him. He is drawn into it in the sense that he feels himself to be overflowing with the delight of closeness to God, and longs to bring something of this to others, thereby consolidating further its hold within his soul as he begins to live in the service of his fellows. On the other hand, as he discovers that the best things in life are within, he finds less and less satisfaction in pursuing those things which the lower reaches of his personality crave: good food, fast cars, power, reputation – the list is familiar.

These two opposing forces do not, in fact, clash, as secular critics of religion would claim; rather they create a new and radical synthesis in the human personality. For the man or woman who is transformed by regular prayer is also undergoing a basic change in his or her social function. No longer is such a person essentially a consumer, sleepily sucking at the teat of the materialist golden calf; instead he shows himself concerned with improving society. This explains why to take a walk down any old street in Cairo or Damascus is to notice not only ancient and imposing mosques, but also public watering fountains, schools, hospitals and aqueducts, which are the direct result of the presence of those mosques.

The life of prayer as understood in Islam is a fundamental challenge to the modern attitude to the individual's role in society, which is defined merely as his contribution to the utilitarian, soulless contract of production and consumption. The Muslim life rises above this mechanical estimate of man, for Islam is founded, as it always has been, on the selfless pursuit of sanctity, and of what is in society's interests, regardless of the possibility of reward.

Hence the Islamic State, wherever it has been established, constitutes a collective social enterprise uniquely different from any other system of government and society known to man. It is not a welfare state, since traditionally most services and public works have been carried out by private organisations and individuals. Neither can it be said to resemble capitalism, for Islamic law does not recognise the principle of unlimited usufruct of land and capital known to Roman law (*jus utendi et abutendi*), which still underlies the theory of Western capitalism. Property belongs to God, and is to be used, with government guidance if necessary, for the benefit of His creatures.

The radical implications of this vision are still being worked out in the Third World, where Islam is the only indigenous ideology. But one thing is clear: where the central economic lubricant is the act of prayer, tremendous and unrivalled freedom must result. Prayer breeds social charity, and the role of the state is restricted to the maintenance of law and order and to the conduct of international relations. Prayer, strange as it may seem, can mean low taxes.

Prayer transforms the state in other realms also. As its influence radiates through society, ethical standards rise. Political irresponsibility and terrorism, the result of selfishness, become uncommon. Delinquency, muggings, suicide, pornography, drug abuse – all the symptoms of a society without God – cannot be treated individually by the pundits of some fashionable "social science". The underlying disease itself, which is the imbalance resulting from the absence of spiritual nourishment, can only be cured by prayer.

At this point we come to another of the characteristic forms of the Muslim life: the payment of the *Zakat*, the obligatory tithe on wealth. In a sense it forms the natural consequence and complement of prayer, the most visible and fixed of the *salat*'s social implications. Muslim almsgiving does not consist primarily in the handing out of banknotes to derelicts in railway stations, although this can be part of it. Neither can it be reduced to the flavourless and abstract gesture of signing a cheque and sending it off to a favourite charity. Rather, the Muslim understands the practice of giving to others from his own wealth and earnings in a far broader sense. His nature, if he has been living in accordance with his religion, is to give out as much as possible and as frequently as he is able. Open the Qur'an to almost any page and you will see this confirmed: wherever God tells His servants to pray He also enjoins upon them the practice of charity. At the very beginning of the Book, at the opening of that stunning overture called *Surat al-Baqara*, we read:

This is the Book in which there is no doubt, a
guidance for the Godfearing;
Those that have faith in the Unseen, and establish
the prayer, and of that which We have
bestowed upon them give out.
Such are they that receive guidance from their
Lord. Such are the triumphant.

In these verses it is clear that God defines those that
fear Him in certain terms: faith in the unseen world,
the observance of the Prayer by which we give
thanks to God for what He has given us, and thirdly,
the giving out again from those same gifts. Thus God
sets out at the opening of His Book a brief yet utterly
comprehensive summary of what the practical
implementation of the Book will engender: faith,
which encourages man to pray, prayer, which
encourages him to give and to serve, and finally,
service, which increases him in faith.

"And of that which We have bestowed upon them
give out." The most obvious implication of this: the
traditional provision of public works by private
individuals. But in addition there is the institution of
the *waqf*, the inalienable endowment, whereby some
commercial project has its profits turned over wholly
or partly to a particular school or hospital in perpet-
uity, either by charter, or through making the
endowment in a written legacy.

Needless to remark, giving to others also exists on
a more modest scale. Not everyone is able to build
and donate a school or a bridge. Begging as a
profession is hateful to Islam, for as the Prophet said,
"The upper hand is better than the lower," yet the

genuinely poor are with us always, even in the most technically advanced industrial countries, and it is our duty to render help whenever we can. Islam teaches that charity should be given secretly, for as the Qur'an tells us, "If you give your charity openly then it is well, but should you hide it, then that is better for you, and will obliterate some of your wrong actions". Similarly we should be gentle and never patronising when we give. God says in the Qur'an: "Do not make your almsgiving valueless by reproach and injury."

Islam distinguishes between two categories of charity: the optional, generally termed *sadaqa*, and the mandatory, the *zakat*. The latter constitutes the necessary revenue for the state, which distributes it into those areas which might have been neglected by the "free market" system of Islamic welfare economics. The Qur'an envisages and lays down certain areas in the economy from which these revenues are to be levied, and also specifies who and what is entitled to benefit from them.

The first, and traditionally the most lucrative area in which the *zakat* is imposed, is the agricultural sector. According to the Qur'an, the landowner (not the farmer himself) is required to pay ten percent of his net profit every year to the state treasury, on condition that the crops grow readily, or that the land is used solely for pasturing. However if his land should be irrigated mechanically, through electric or diesel pumps (to give the modern equivalent), or with artesian wells, or if the land is benefitting from a hydro-electric scheme operating outside the farm itself, this rate is reduced to five percent. The differential is to encourage efficient farming.

Elsewhere in the economy different rates of *zakat* are levied. The Islamic fiscal system is based on a gold standard, that is, the Islamic currency is readily convertible to gold or silver at a fixed rate which may only be raised or lowered by central bank directives approved by the head of state. Every transaction becomes liable to a one-fortieth *zakat* tax payable on its value in gold and silver. The tax is assessed at the end of the financial year, and replaces the Western system of "income tax". In addition, *zakat* is assessed at the same rate, or *nisba*, on capital gains, including bequests and gifts, and return on shares in private corporations, and is also payable on all wealth held in money form including private bank accounts.

The third and last principal species of *zakat* is of particular interest. It falls due on gross profits from the exploitation of natural resources, including mines and oil wells. Covering revenue from all these sources the *zakat* rate rises to 20 percent, discouraging unnecessary waste of non-renewable minerals and energy sources. Renewable sources of energy, such as hydroelectric projects and solar energy, are encouraged by being taxed at the substantially lower rate of five percent.

According to classical authorities in the field of Islamic economics, *zakat* collection and distribution is to be accomplished with the minimum number of employees. Local town clerks, solicitors or accountants calculate the taxable sections of their local community's economy, and when necessary check up the individual tax assessment and returns of the citizens. The local authorities are then entitled to redistribute a certain proportion of this revenue within the area under their jurisdiction, and then pass on the rest to the central government, which in turn channels it into the sectors which do not receive private funds, namely, the armed forces, the police and the judiciary.

From what has just been said it is clear that Islamic welfare economics is characterised by great simplicity. It reveals the central pillar of Islamic political thought, which is that the state has only a very limited role to play, interfering in its citizen's affairs only when absolutely necessary. Otherwise the Muslim polity is self-sustaining, relying on the fundamental sense of responsibility which religion mediates to its members.

The other side of the *zakat* equation, which concerns those sectors of society entitled to state assistance, divides into eight areas. First among those who receive a share of the *zakat* are the poor, and in particular those who are in danger of losing their lives as a result of simply not finding enough to eat. According to the World Health Organisation, eight million of our fellow men and women die of starvation each year throughout the globe. Aid to these people takes precedence over any other use which might be made of *zakat* funds.

The second area of disbursement is made up of those people within the boundaries of the Islamic state who are not in any immediate danger of starvation but who nevertheless live well below the poverty line. The government is entitled to distribute *zakat* funds to such people, especially by providing them with the means to begin a career, for example in the form of education grants, or assistance with buying agriculture equipment.

Thirdly, mention should be made of the expenses incurred unavoidably in the collection and distribution of the *zakat* itself. It is traditional in the Islamic world that *zakat* workers are voluntary, but if such labour is not forthcoming, or if it proves necessary to buy documenting equipment such as a computer, then the *zakat* fund itself may be used to defray expenses. It is perhaps useful to recall here in parentheses that other government officials, including the head of state himself, are not entitled to government funds at all, but must ensure that they have sufficient income from other sources, before they opt to enter the world of politics which is a world of service, not of personal gain.

Fourthly, there exists a special facility in the state treasury with regard to what is now in effect an extinct category: slaves. Islam prohibits slavery in the form which is familiar to students of European and American history. But in times of war there nevertheless exists a special mechanism for integrating prisoners of war. Rather than holding enemy troops in camps Islam allows that those who are of good behaviour may be sent for public service in the homes of private citizens. But in time of peace there is no such means of acquiring bonded servants, hence there is no permanent population of non-free people in an Islamic state. This system is called in Islamic law the "law of indenture". In order to secure their release from their service, or from the prisoner-of-war camps themselves, these bonded servants are entitled to apply for assistance from the *zakat* fund to compensate the households which they are leaving.

Fifthly, the *zakat* treasury receives applications for

assistance from people in chronic debt. After investigating the request the treasury is entitled to pay off such debts if it is clear that the debtor is never likely to be in a position to do so himself.

Sixthly comes a general category of public service. From the *zakat* fund, and once the foregoing categories have received their due, the head of the treasury may order disbursements upon projects of general benefit, including the provision of infrastructure not furnished by the private sector. The armed forces are likewise provided for from this category.

Seventhly, money may be sent overseas as foreign aid over and above the mandatory expenditures mentioned in the first of the eight categories.

Finally there is a small category, historically of great importance, which provides for travellers who lack the means to return home. A voyager or tourist in a state where Islamic law is applied has a statutory right, should he lose his money (for example) to contact the local administration and request a ticket to his country of origin.

The implementation of Islamic welfare economics has historically proved highly successful. Often the funds of the Caliphate were deployed in every one of the eight categories we have just mentioned. Far from being idealistic or divorced from reality, the Islamic vision of a society based on service has regularly been put into effect. In the golden centuries of Muslim civilisation free private sector education resulted in a literacy rate of over fifty percent, a figure which only began to decline during the period of colonial domination. When the armies of the Reconquest entered Cordoba, the erstwhile capital of Muslim Spain, they were astonished to find a city provided with street lighting at night, and possessed of over four hundred public baths and a great library containing over half a million books.

So prosperous was Islamic civilisation under Muslim economic law that a voluminous body of records details events such as the following, which seem quite incredible today: a contemporary account records an exchange of correspondence between the devout eighth-century caliph Umar ibn Abdal Aziz and his governor over the province of Iraq. The governor had complained in one letter as follows: "Commander of the Faithful! I have given from the treasury to all in need, but some money still remains." The Caliph replied: "Seek out all those that have contracted reasonable debts, and pay off what they owe." The governor then wrote back, saying: "I have paid off every debt, but we still have a surplus." "Seek out every unmarried person," the Caliph told him, "who has insufficient money to marry, and pay their dowries and get them married." "I have already done so," came the reply, "but we still have a surplus." Finally the Caliph sent him the following message: "Find out everyone who has to pay taxes and absolve him from paying them, for we have enough money for a year or two."

Economics, then, is just as much a subject of religious concern as are theology and the rites of worship. In the all-embracing world view of Islam no distinction is drawn between the religious and the secular; rather, all of human existence must reflect the presence of God. But let us now narrow the compass a little again, and return to the fundamental acts of devotion which serve thus to transform every other dimension of the Muslim life. "Islam is built on five pillars", of which we have examined so far the doctrine, as enshrined in the two Testimonies, the formal prayer, and the *zakat* tithe. Two other pillars remain.

Many people are aware that Muslims observe an annual fast, during the month of Ramadan. Why they do so, however, is not always so well known. Of course, fasting, in the various forms men have observed it through history, is known to have beneficial effects on one's health. But in a religious context it is primarily a technique of seeking proximity to God. In a sense it is a counterpart to prayer: prayer constitutes an addition to our lives, while fasting is – visibly at any rate – a subtraction, for by it we are advised to avoid certain things during a certain period. The relation between the two is subtle and only becomes clear with time.

The Qur'an says: "O you who believe! Fasting is prescribed for you, as it was prescribed for those before you, that perhaps you may learn self-restraint". Numerous examples of "those before you" spring to mind; in fact it seems that every religious dispensation before Islam knew the practice of fasting in one form or another.

The archaic practices of Hinduism conserve for us an interesting picture of fasting in ancient times. There were certain days of the year set aside for fasting by women, and others for men. In our day, the Brahmin caste in India still observe a complete abstinence from food and drink on the eleventh and twelfth days of every Hindu month.

Fasting was also known to the ancient Egyptians and Greeks. Similarly, the ancient scriptures of Persia advocate fasting and affirm its value as a means of spiritual purification. The Jews of the Old Testament were known to observe fasts on days of danger and misfortune, and on several fixed days in their calendar, of which the best known to non-Jews is the fast of Yom Kippur.

Jesus is said to have fasted forty days and nights before his final entry into Jerusalem. The early Christians, most of whom observed the Mosaic law, also fasted on the Day of Atonement. But as history rolled on, less emphasis was placed on exact adherence to the practices observed by Jesus, and the Lenten fast assumed a largely symbolic role, involving an abstention from certain types of food only.

Fasting, then, is as old as religion itself. When Islam appeared, its scripture acknowledged and continued this ancient practice. The Qur'an taught the early Muslims to fast on any day, but stated that as a minimum they were to observe the month-long fast of Ramadan. Later on, religious authors spoke of three grades of fasting: firstly, the "outward fast", where one abstains from food, drink, and sex; secondly, the fast of the senses and the tongue, whereby one is to avoid looking at or hearing anything which might turn the attention to material things, and where the fasting person keeps from backbiting and hostile language; and thirdly, the highest grade of fasting, the "fast of the soul", where the above practices are perfected by an abstinence from any thought which might impair one's awareness of God's presence.

The basic, mandatory elements of the Muslim fast, however, are straightforward. As the Qur'an and the teachings of the Prophet expound it, it consists in the simple abstention from food, drink, and sexual relations during the hours of daylight. Just before the call for the Dawn Prayer is given, the Muslims gather to share the meal called *suhur*, usually a light meal of vegetables, yoghurt and fruit. Then, after the prayer, they fast through the day until sunset, when they take another meal ending the day's fast.

Because the Muslim calendar is derived from the phases of the moon, the fasting month falls a little earlier each year. The effect of this is to balance out the discrepancy between fasting in the northern and the southern hemispheres. It is often thought that in certain parts of the globe the fast will be easier than in others, for the length of the day, as well as its temperature, varies from season to season and from land to land. But Ramadan, creeping forwards at a rate of about ten days in each solar year, ensures that wherever one may be on the face of the planet the fast will fall sometimes in winter, and sometimes in summer. Similarly, although in high latitudes the days can be long, there is no heat. A balance thus obtains, so that fasting is similarly efficacious all over the world. And as regards the Muslims who live in those extreme latitudes where the sun rises and sets only once a year (there is an ancient Muslim community in Finland, for example), they simply adhere to the timetable of the nearest major town south of the Arctic Circle.

Thus the daylong fast is never a real physical trial. But there remains the problem of the bodily ill, the elderly, and those whose work involves strenuous physical labour. Here, too, the moderation which is the watchword of Islam has intervened. According to the Qur'an anyone sick or engaged upon a journey is entitled not to observe the fast, and no blame attaches to this. The days in which the fast is broken are made up at any later time during the year when the sickness is at an end or when the traveller returns. As for the elderly, or the incurably ill, such people are neither required to observe the fast nor to make it up afterwards. Those working at tasks which are physically demanding such as quarrymen or steel workers, are likewise permitted to break the fast, together with certain other categories of people, such as pregnant women. The guiding principle, as with every other practice of Islam, is that what cannot be done, or causes hardship, is not required.

The benefits of fasting are well known to those who have practiced any traditional religion. To have fasted is to understand why it is so important, and why in the Muslim world so many people choose to observe the non-obligatory fasts as well as the month of Ramadan. However, Ramadan is revered as the most blessed month of the year, the month in which the Qur'an was revealed to Muhammad, God's final Prophet on this earth. It is a time of grace and spiritual energy, when the acts of worship practiced throughout the year suddenly take on new and urgent meaning. Towards the close of this month comes the Night of Power, the *Laylat al-Qadr*, which, as the Qur'an relates, is "better than a thousand months". Preceded by almost an entire month of fasting and supererogatory prayer, this night is marked by spending it in prayer and reciting the Qur'an. The Prophet stressed that it is a time for spiritual effort and breakthrough; and according to tradition it was the night when God proclaimed man's status as His deputy on the earth, thereby raising him above all other creatures: it is the moment when man can most easily become himself.

It is essential to try to understand the effects of fasting on the human spirit. Muslims say that when they fast they feel that a barrier has been erected between them and the world. No longer are they constantly absorbing sustenance from their surroundings. One of the effects of this is to compel them to realise their total dependence upon food and drink, so that they fervently thank their Creator for His unfailing provision of their daily needs.

In addition, they will come to know hunger. We read so often that one-quarter of the world's population is in a state of constant hunger, yet how many of us realise the true nature of this sensation? If our lunch is two hours late most of us feel extremely uncomfortable. But to grasp the true meaning of hunger it is necessary to go without food for longer. By the end of his day's fasting the Muslim usually feels hungry, but not unbearably so. Thus we are awakened in the most real and direct way to the plight of millions of our fellow human beings, and will be more ready to extend to them our assistance.

However, fasting has another, far more transformative effect. It engenders a sense of detachment from the world. Physical separation, as a powerful symbol, brings about in the mind and the heart that appreciation of distance which is one of the states most cherished by spiritual seekers everywhere. When fasting, the Muslim acts with a new sense of confidence, able more fully to concentrate his attention on his material as well as his spiritual life. Temporarily despairing of food and drink, he is able to devote himself more fully to the One Who is the source of all his sustenance.

Thus, during Ramadan, the Muslim finds that his religious life takes on new meaning. The Qur'an yields up new secrets and treasures; in fact, every devotional practice functions more efficiently during the fasting months. Thus the optional acts of worship are practiced more consistently, until the whole day becomes infused with religious meaning. This is why in Ramadan Muslims spend long hours in prayer. They strive to obey God in everything they do, endeavouring to please Him by visiting relatives and the sick, by serving the neighbourhood in some way, and by avoiding even more than usual any act of injustice or dishonesty.

Ramadan is thus traditionally the time of reconciliation, of love and forgiveness, as well as of spiritual ascent. It purifies the soul and whole communities of the misdeeds and misunderstandings of the past year, and acts as a powerful energy for reform, so that when the month is over, and the season of festivals begins, the Muslim may face the future with new determination and strength, repentant for his former bad habits and resolute that he will never again return to them. Thus, men and women, and whole societies purify themselves during this month, which becomes the turning point of the year, and – for many people – of their lives.

Three months after Ramadan comes the season of the great Pilgrimage to Mecca. Towards that city and its Sacred Precincts an ever-increasing number of men and women converge each year, from every possible corner of the earth, to don two simple white cloths and to follow one set of rites for a few days in an impressive display of Islam's disregard for racial or national divisions. Each year over three million people make the pilgrimage, making it the largest temporary gathering of humanity on the globe.

As we have stated, there exist certain methods of worship which are common to every religion: we have mentioned prayer, almsgiving, and fasting. To these should also be added the act of making pilgrimage. Many people believe that it has been God's will as He has unfolded history to give preference to certain places and to certain times. Although people and peoples pass away, God's earth and its geography remain. Thus, certain places honoured and blessed by the presence of great Prophets and saints can be of benefit to us long after those people have gone. For it is a Muslim belief that where the light of God descends upon a certain person, whether in the form of a revelation founding a new religion, or as a lesser spiritual opening to one of His Saints, a trace of that light remains for those who are able to see it. This force, which Muslims call *baraka*, historically transforms certain spots into busy centres of pilgrimage and devotion for later generations.

In this spirit, Judaism know the pilgrimage to Jerusalem, city of the patriarchs and prophets, and blessed site of revelation and worship. According to the Torah, every male, adult, physically fit Jew must complete the pilgrimage to the holy city, bringing with him an offering. The rites of pilgrimage were set for certain specific days in the year.

Pilgrimage in early Christianity followed the same pattern. As other influences made themselves felt, however, and as the faith expanded, pilgrimages were also instituted to the Holy See at Rome, and to the regional tombs of saints such as St. Thomas at Canterbury and Santiago de Compostela in Spain.

We meet with much the same picture in the context of the Oriental religions. On the banks of the sacred river Ganges hundreds of thousands of Indians bathe to purify themselves from vice and evil. Buddhists of both major schools emphasise the importance of the pilgrimage to the town of Kia in Bengal, where the Buddha began his life of devotion and sanctity.

Islam, then, in instituting a system of pilgrimage, does not differ with the religions God revealed for earlier ages, but although it recommends paying visits to the burial places of great saints, it is unique in laying such central emphasis on one great collective event. The Hajj, the journey to the sacred places in and around Mecca, is an act of recollection and worship, but it is also a symbolic act representing the spirit's return to its homeland: one of the central elements of the Muslim life.

Let us start our visit to the Hajj at the international airport at the Red Sea port of Jeddah, where most pilgrims now arrive. Making our way through the customs formalities we are already struck by an indefinable atmosphere of excitement and purpose hanging in the air. Emerging into the bright sunlight of the city itself this impression is confirmed. Already a number of pilgrims have donned the traditional clothing necessary for the Hajj: for men, a waist-wrapper covering the body between the shins and the naval, and another piece of cloth, again of seamless white, cast over the shoulder. Women are dressed, usually in white, from head to foot, leaving the face and the hands exposed. The effect is instant and remarkable. One moment there disembarks an aeroplane full of Moroccan businessmen, Ugandan peasants, or Indonesian traders; the next, all distinctions of culture and wealth are stripped away: all are equal, dressed in the uniform and timeless white of the Hajj.

The same day we take a bus for the seventy mile journey inland across the bare hills of western Arabia to the Holy City itself. At a point just outside the outskirts there is a checkpoint, beyond which no non-Muslims are allowed to pass. The reason for this is obvious: Mecca is a city for worship and devotion, and the presence of tourists at the holy sites would be insufferable, a profane distraction of the worst kind.

Slowly, we drive through the wide yet crowded streets of the little city. Our fellow passengers have already begun the *talbiya*, a litany God taught Muhammad during his final pilgrimage, a paean of thanksgiving and praise which is intensified until the gates of the Holy Mosque are sighted. Here we leave the bus, and cross the street to filter slowly through the expectant crowds into the Sacred Precincts. Here at last we can see before us the Ka'ba, the blank cubic building draped in black cloth, built so many years ago by Abraham and his son Ishmael for the worship of Almighty God.

Upon entering the Precincts we begin to make the prescribed circuits of the House, seven times: an act of seeking God's forgiveness and of deriving spiritual power from the House. Then we proceed to the valley of Mina, where many pilgrims spend the night.

The following day we walk or drive to the plain of Arafat, a distance of about ten miles. Here we rest in a great city of tents, and pray to God to forgive us our wrong actions at the Mountain of Mercy, the Jabal al-Rahma, which stands at the epicentre of the vast plain. Following this, we make haste to the area of Muzdalifa, another of the sacred points, and then return to Mecca, where we repeat the seven circuits, and walk between the two hills of Safa and Marwa, again seven times, in commemoration of the quest of Hagar and Ishmael for water; another gesture replete with symbolic meaning. Then we spend two or three days in contemplation at Mina, where there are certain other rites to be observed.

To understand the inner significance of the Hajj ceremonies it is necessary to remember that Mecca is in many respects a town apart from all others. Good actions and bad are more clearly discerned, and the reward or punishment for them is held to be proportionately greater. Within the limits of the city fighting and all aggressiveness are forbidden. No pilgrim is allowed for any reason to harm a human being, an animal or a bird during his sojourn in the city. In the state of *ihram*, the special state the pilgrim enters into when he puts on the dress of the rites, he feels that he is ridding himself for a while of all that linked him to his former life, with its desires and enmities, and can now devote his attention wholeheartedly to his Creator.

The circuits around the Ka'ba themselves symbolise the circulation of the heart around the holiness of God. In the same vein, the running between the two hills of Safa and Marwa in the great hall now built to enclose them suggests moving between the two aspects of God's mercy, compassion and acceptance.

The culminating point of the Hajj is the most simple rite of all. Here millions of people stand together in a scene of great beauty, surrounded by mountains on all sides. As the hours pass, one's thoughts, already focused on God by days of uninterrupted worship, have time to look deeply into one's life. What have we done in the service of God and humanity? What recurrent weaknesses must we strive to combat? Whom have we wronged? What is holding us back from the purity which is the prerequisite of spiritual knowledge? And at the same time another symbolism inherent in the psychology of the Hajj becomes clear. Standing on the plain of Arafat we cannot but remember the day on which God will resurrect us together with all mankind, when the time of repentance will be irrevocably past. Now, however, there still remains a path back to the world, for soon we will be going home: an opportunity to set our lives right before we die to await the Day of Judgement.

Returning to our homes after days of physical exhaustion and spiritual uplift we are radically transfigured. The overpowering sense of contrition and repentance which we bring back with us is visible

immediately to all who know us. The Hajj, culmination of the Muslim life, as it builds up from
frequent prayers, to annual fasts, to the once-in-a-
lifetime experience of pilgrimage, has transformed
another soul.

Postface

At every point through this little book we have tried to show that behind every outward form in the Islamic religion there lies an inward significance and a spiritual impact. But it is just as true to say that it is our inward states which in turn condition the outward forms of worship which have been taught us – as we believe – by God. This is one key sense of the Qur'an's characterisation of Islam as "the middle way": balancing in this fashion, it is neither easy nor difficult; neither formal and superficial nor esoteric and elitist.

In our present century we are only too familiar with the presence of imbalance. Our sports cars, holidays and pension plans: all the status symbols of the modern manner of living, seem tasteless and without meaning. The reason is understood intuitively by many, but few know how to respond: we have lost contact with the mystery which lies within ourselves; we have forgotten what we are.

Science cannot tell us how to live. "The blank space in the modern heart," said scientist Julian Huxley, "is a God-shaped blank." And life without the transcendent is not only desultory and without meaning, it is miserable, as the Qur'an tells us. We can only become robots, anaesthetised by television, drink and our leisure preoccupations if we fail to hear the insistent inquiry of the Qur'an: "Where, then, are you going?" Religion, far from being a harmless and eccentric hobby, or the refuge of outrageous fanatics, is in its most intact form the sole path to finding the answer to this question. Finding, not giving – for the tools in the Muslim devotional inventory are not in themselves the answer, rather they will, when properly used, show us not only how to know, but also how to feel, see, and in the reallest possible sense, to be the answer.

Islam, then, is no opiate. It concerns itself with the next life, true, but never is this concern seen as immaterial to the pressing problems and needs of the world into which we have been born. For it injects energy into a system in the grip of entropy, it makes human life a source of giving rather than of endless acquisition. This force spreads out from the heart into society through channels engineered with this purpose in view. Religion, for the Muslim, is a full-time activity: the mosque leads both to a life in harmony with the world, and to submission to God.

One last remark. The reader may already have guessed why, despite its principles, the Islamic world is in its present state of disarray. The sad answer is that what we call the world of Islam is in reality something rather different. Although the Muslim religion seems to be the most living of the world's great faiths, it is nevertheless not immune to the deadening modern disease of materialism and greed. Its geography shattered into over forty fragments by the colonial powers of the last century, those who lay claim to it are only just beginning to regain their former sense of unity and purpose. Yet despite all the odds, Islam regrows in its traditional homelands, and now also in expanding communities in the West. Its future in our age seems bright. Amidst the ruins of a thousand faiths and secular ideologies, Islam, religion of life, lives on.